EASY SIMULATIONS

American Revolution

by Renay M. Scott, Ph.D.

New York • Toronto • London • Auckland • Sydney
Mexico City • New Delhi • Hong Kong • Buenos Aires

Teaching Resources

Editors: Tim Bailey, Maria L. Chang
Cover design by Jason Robinson
Cover illustration by Doug Knutson
Interior design by Holly Grundon
Interior illustrations by Kathie Kelleher

ISBN-13: 978-0-439-52221-2
ISBN-10: 0-439-52221-8
Copyright © 2007 by Renay Scott
All rights reserved.
Printed in the U.S.A.

4 5 6 7 8 9 10   40   15 14 13 12 11

Contents

Welcome to *Easy Simulations: American Revolution*. Using simulations in the classroom is one of the most powerful teaching methods you can choose. Students learn most when they see a purpose to an activity, are engaged in the learning process, and are having fun. Children love to role-play, and they do it naturally. How often have you overheard them say something like, "O.K., you be the bad guy, and I'll be the good guy"? Why not tap into students' imaginations and creativity and teach them by engaging them in a simulation?

What Is a Simulation?

A simulation is a teacher-directed, student-driven activity that provides lifelike problem-solving experiences through role-playing or reenacting. Simulations use an incredible range of powerful teaching strategies. Students will acquire a richness and depth of understanding of history impossible to gain through the use of any textbook. They will take responsibility for their own learning, discover that they must work cooperatively with their team in order to succeed, and learn that they must apply skills in logic to solve the problems that they encounter. You will find that this simulation addresses a variety of academic content areas and fully integrates them into this social studies activity. In addition, simulations motivate *all* of your students to participate because what they're required to do will be fully supported by their teammates and you.

History Comes Alive

The American Revolution simulation is designed to teach students about this important period of history by inviting them to relive that event. Over the course of five days, they will recreate some of the experiences of the people who were beginning a new nation. By taking the perspective of a historical character living through the event, students will begin to see that history is so much more than just names, dates, and places, but rather, real experiences of people like themselves.

Briefly, students will find out what it was like to live as a colonist in the late 1700s in Lexington, Massachusetts. After choosing a profession, they will discover that life in colonial Lexington is about to change dramatically. In the War for Independence, students will have to choose whether to stay loyal to England's King George III or rebel against him and start their own country. They will live through some of the most important events in the American Revolution and finally, participate in the British surrender at Yorktown.

Throughout all these events, students will keep a diary of their experiences and use their problem-solving skills to deal with challenges they will encounter. At the end of the simulation, they will write a final diary entry, describing what they have learned during the simulation. You can use this diary as an ongoing assessment tool to determine what students are learning.

Everything You Need

This book provides an easy-to-use guide for running this five-day simulation—everything you need to create an educational experience that your students will talk about for a very long time. You will find background information for both yourself and your students that describes the history and significance of the American Revolution. You'll also find authentic accounts—letters and journals—of people who were alive during this pivotal time in history, as well as maps, charts, illustrations, and reproducible student journal pages. Engaging extension activities can be used during the simulation or as a supplement to your own American Revolution unit.

Before you begin the simulation, be certain to read through the entire book so you can familiarize yourself with how a simulation works and prepare any materials that you may need. Feel free to supplement with photos, illustrations, video, music, and any other details that will enhance the experience for you and your students. Enjoy!

SETTING THE SCENE:
The American Revolution

By the mid-1700s, life in the American colonies had settled into a comfortable rhythm. For the most part, the colonists had been allowed to govern themselves. Britain's attention was elsewhere—it had been engaged in a war with France over vast territories in America for several years. But with the end of the French and Indian War in 1763, things were about to change for the colonists. The war that had gained Britain much of the land once held by France proved to be quite costly. To help pay its debt from the war, Britain passed a series of acts (laws) that taxed the colonists.

In 1764, the British Parliament passed the Revenue Act, known as the Sugar Act in the colonies. The law placed a tax on molasses entering the colonies. The following year, Britain passed the Quartering Act, requiring colonists to help pay for housing the British soldiers stationed in the colonies. Around the same time, the controversial Stamp Act was also passed. This law placed a tax on marriage licenses, newspapers, and 47 other documents. These taxes angered the colonists, who protested that they didn't have a say in the law. They had no vote in the British Parliament and complained that this was "taxation without representation." They started forming secret groups called the "Sons of Liberty," who met to find a way to oppose the Stamp Act. Colonists began to take sides. Those who agreed with Britain were called Loyalists, and those who opposed were called Patriots.

Attributes

Attributes are the numbers that make each role unique. The attributes are Military Expertise, Common Sense, Stamina, Negotiating Skills, Loyalty, and Morale. Throughout the simulation, attribute numbers will be used during "skill spins" to resolve various situations that the groups will encounter. Players spin the spinner (page 23) and compare the number they spun to their attribute number to decide whether their attempt at solving a problem is successful or not. For example, say a student's character is trying to forage for food during the harsh winter at Valley Forge. If the number he spins is equal to or lower than his Common Sense number, then he has succeeded in finding food.

An attribute check can be made only once per person per situation. In other words, if a student fails in his Common Sense skill spin then that person cannot attempt to forage again. Someone else would have to try his or her luck by making another Common Sense skill spin.

Below is a description of the various Attributes:

Military Expertise: How skilled a character is at being a soldier. Some men had formal training in the army during the French and Indian War as colonial militia (minutemen), and some had no training at all.

Common Sense: A person's wisdom and ability to understand and reason. This can be very important in figuring out how to react to different situations and foreseeing problems.

Stamina: How much physical and mental endurance a character has. For instance, it would be used to determine how well a colonist can withstand hunger, fatigue, or cold.

Negotiating Skills: How well a character can reason with or influence other people.

Loyalty: A person's sense of commitment to a particular cause or way of thinking.

Morale: How strongly a character feels about his or her choice to be a Patriot or Loyalist. A high number indicates a colonist who strongly believes that she is right in her decision to either support or rebel against the king. A low number indicates a person who is second-guessing his decision and might decide to go over to the other side. Of all the attributes, this is the only number that changes throughout the simulation. The Morale number is set apart from the other attributes on the student's character sheet. At times students will be called upon to spin for their Morale. If they spin their Morale number or lower, then they continue with the side that they are currently on. But if they spin a higher number, then they must spin their Loyalty attribute number or lower to stay on the same side.

SETTING THE SCENE:
The American Revolution

By the mid-1700s, life in the American colonies had settled into a comfortable rhythm. For the most part, the colonists had been allowed to govern themselves. Britain's attention was elsewhere—it had been engaged in a war with France over vast territories in America for several years. But with the end of the French and Indian War in 1763, things were about to change for the colonists. The war that had gained Britain much of the land once held by France proved to be quite costly. To help pay its debt from the war, Britain passed a series of acts (laws) that taxed the colonists.

In 1764, the British Parliament passed the Revenue Act, known as the Sugar Act in the colonies. The law placed a tax on molasses entering the colonies. The following year, Britain passed the Quartering Act, requiring colonists to help pay for housing the British soldiers stationed in the colonies. Around the same time, the controversial Stamp Act was also passed. This law placed a tax on marriage licenses, newspapers, and 47 other documents. These taxes angered the colonists, who protested that they didn't have a say in the law. They had no vote in the British Parliament and complained that this was "taxation without representation." They started forming secret groups called the "Sons of Liberty," who met to find a way to oppose the Stamp Act. Colonists began to take sides. Those who agreed with Britain were called Loyalists, and those who opposed were called Patriots.

THE AMERICAN REVOLUTION (CONTINUED)

Disappointed over the colonists' response to the earlier laws, Charles Townshend took over the job of raising money for Britain. He enacted another series of laws called the Townshend Acts in 1767. These laws included new taxes on lead, paint, paper, glass, and tea imported to the colonies. In protest, the colonists boycotted (refused to buy) these goods. In addition, they started attacking public officials like the governor and tax collectors. Britain responded by sending troops to keep order in 1768.

The colonists resented the growing number of British troops. Tension was rising. In March 1770, a group of colonists gathered near a customs house that British soldiers were guarding. The colonists mocked the troops and began throwing snowballs at them. Someone yelled, "Fire!" and shots rang out. Even though the British soldiers were under orders not to shoot, they did, and five colonists died. This event became known as the Boston Massacre.

Hostility between Britain and the colonists escalated over the next three years. In 1773, a group of Patriots who were tired of the tax on tea decided to make a statement. Late on the night of December 16th, the Patriots, disguised as Indians, crept toward the Boston Harbor. They boarded three ships loaded with tea from Britain and tossed more than 300 chests of tea into the Boston Harbor. The Boston Tea Party, as it became known, greatly angered England's King George III, and he dispatched even more troops to the colonies in 1774. The colonists persisted with their boycotts and written protests in newspapers. As a new year dawns, relations between England and the colonies are reaching the breaking point.

Easy Simulations: American Revolution © 2007 by Renay Scott, Scholastic Teaching Resources

Organizing and Managing the Simulation

Before students embark on their exciting five-day experience, you'll need to set the stage for the simulation. First, make photocopies of the reproducible pages at the end of this section:

- Life in the Colonies (pages 16–17)

- Choose a Role (page 18)

- A Colonist's Diary and journal page (pages 19–20)

- Rubrics (pages 21–22)

- Simulation Spinner (page 23)

Explain to students that they will be recreating history, using the simulation and their imaginations to learn what it was like to be an American colonist during the Revolutionary War. They will be taking on the roles of different colonists in that time period and making the same decisions that those colonists made.

Distribute copies of "Life in the Colonies" to students. You might also want to reproduce the page on a transparency to display on the overhead projector. Together, read the selection to build students' background knowledge about the time period they're about to live through. Then divide the class into three groups. These three groups will represent the divisions that existed among the colonists in 1774. One group will be the Patriots, another the Loyalists, and the last group will represent the Undecided Citizens.

Choosing a Role

After you have divided the class into three groups, distribute the "Choose a Role" handout, which describes the various roles students can play. Invite students to select a role from the handout, explaining that these "roles" are typical occupations in the New England colonies. Each role comes with its own set of special skills, with strengths and weaknesses indicated by a number ranging from 1 to 5. These numbers are called Attributes. The higher the attribute number, the more able the character. (See Attributes, next page.) The Morale number indicates how confident a character is in the choice he or she has made to support the king or rebel against Britain. Morale can change throughout the simulation.

Encourage students within each group to choose a variety of roles to make the simulation more interesting. After students have chosen a role to play in the simulation, they will get a chance to develop their characters more fully and learn what it was like to be a colonist living in Lexington in 1774. They will do this in Episode 1 (page 24).

Attributes

Attributes are the numbers that make each role unique. The attributes are Military Expertise, Common Sense, Stamina, Negotiating Skills, Loyalty, and Morale. Throughout the simulation, attribute numbers will be used during "skill spins" to resolve various situations that the groups will encounter. Players spin the spinner (page 23) and compare the number they spun to their attribute number to decide whether their attempt at solving a problem is successful or not. For example, say a student's character is trying to forage for food during the harsh winter at Valley Forge. If the number he spins is equal to or lower than his Common Sense number, then he has succeeded in finding food.

An attribute check can be made only once per person per situation. In other words, if a student fails in his Common Sense skill spin then that person cannot attempt to forage again. Someone else would have to try his or her luck by making another Common Sense skill spin.

Below is a description of the various Attributes:

Military Expertise: How skilled a character is at being a soldier. Some men had formal training in the army during the French and Indian War as colonial militia (minutemen), and some had no training at all.

Common Sense: A person's wisdom and ability to understand and reason. This can be very important in figuring out how to react to different situations and foreseeing problems.

Stamina: How much physical and mental endurance a character has. For instance, it would be used to determine how well a colonist can withstand hunger, fatigue, or cold.

Negotiating Skills: How well a character can reason with or influence other people.

Loyalty: A person's sense of commitment to a particular cause or way of thinking.

Morale: How strongly a character feels about his or her choice to be a Patriot or Loyalist. A high number indicates a colonist who strongly believes that she is right in her decision to either support or rebel against the king. A low number indicates a person who is second-guessing his decision and might decide to go over to the other side. Of all the attributes, this is the only number that changes throughout the simulation. The Morale number is set apart from the other attributes on the student's character sheet. At times students will be called upon to spin for their Morale. If they spin their Morale number or lower, then they continue with the side that they are currently on. But if they spin a higher number, then they must spin their Loyalty attribute number or lower to stay on the same side.

Keeping a Journal

After students have chosen their roles, distribute copies of "A Colonist's Diary" pages—one copy of the cover page and six copies of the blank Dear Diary page. Explain to students that they will be recording their experiences during the simulation in their diaries on a daily basis. To give the diaries a more realistic look, have students use a sheet of 12-by-18-inch brown construction paper or a large brown paper grocery bag for the cover. Demonstrate how to "sew" the journal pages inside the cover page using a hole punch and yarn, as shown below.

On the cover page, have students fill in information about the character they've chosen—their assumed name, role, allegiance (i.e., Loyalist, Patriot, Undecided Citizen), and attribute numbers. When writing in their diary pages, have students

A student's diary often yields rich insights into the student's understanding of historical events and how they impacted ordinary citizens' lives. Use these diaries as your primary tool for assessing students' participation and evaluating how well they understand the simulation's content. (See Assessing and Evaluating, page 15.)

A Colonist's Diary

Student Page

Student's Name: _____ Sandra Barker _____

Colonist's Name and Role: _____ Pete / Farmer _____

Colonist's Allegiance (circle one):   Loyalist   Patriot   (Undecided Citizen)

Colonist's Attributes:

Military Expertise: _____ 4 _____

Common Sense: _____ 3 _____

Stamina: _____ 4 _____

Negotiating Skills: _____ 1 _____

Loyalty: _____ 3 _____

MORALE: _____ 4 _____
(This number may be adjusted throughout the simulation.)

Easy Simulations: American Revolution   19

Date: April 19, 1775

Dear Diary,
Today I saw a friend of mine shot dead by the British! It happened in the village green this morning. We had heard that the British were coming to Lexington to arrest some of the Patriot leaders and capture war supplies hidden in town. But when the soldiers got here they found Patriot minutemen waiting for them! There was some shouting and then all of a sudden they were shooting at each other! I hid behind a stone wall and waited for the shooting to stop. That is when I saw my friend lying on the ground. He had been shot! I have always been undecided whether to stay loyal to the king or support the Patriots but now I think I might join the Patriots!
Pete

record the date of the simulation, not the actual date. For example, use April 19, 1775, rather than November 6, 2007. Students should record the events in that day's episode. Encourage them to write their diary entry "in character," as if the events were really happening to them. This activity gives students the opportunity to take on another person's perspective and experience history as such.

Conducting the Simulation

This simulation is divided into five episodes—one for each day of the school week—each re-creating key events in the American Revolution. Consider starting the simulation on a Monday so that it will run its course by Friday. Complete all preparatory work (e.g., building background knowledge, choosing a character, etc.) during the prior week. Each episode should take about 50–70 minutes, depending on your class size.

The simulation opens with students in the town of Lexington, Massachusetts, in 1774, just before the first battles of the American Revolution. Students will start by conducting research about the life and culture of the colonies during the 1770s. Once cast into character with an understanding of colonial society, students will experience the Battles of Lexington and Concord, the proclamation of independence by colonists, winter at Valley Forge, and the surrender at Yorktown. By the end of the simulation, students will have "participated" in events that happened from 1774 to 1781.

In between each event, students will learn more about life in colonial America, the course of the War for Independence, and the various groups of people affected by the war. The simulation includes the following five episodes:

Episode 1: Before the Storm

Episode 2: The Shot Heard Round the World

Episode 3: Declaring Independence

Episode 4: Winter at Valley Forge

Episode 5: Yorktown

Each episode starts with background information, which puts the event students are about to simulate in context. The episode also features a scenario and an activity. The scenarios present problem-solving situations that re-create some of the events during the Revolution. The activities are research opportunities designed to enhance students' understanding of life in America at this time in history. These activities often require students to conduct research on the Internet. In the Resources section at the back of the book, we provide Web sites that have been researched, are historically accurate, and are student-friendly. (*NOTE: Always check the links PRIOR to letting students access them on the Internet as the content of Web sites tends to change over time.) You might choose to skip the activities and have students conduct all their research at the beginning of the unit before starting the simulation. Building background knowledge before engaging in the simulation will enrich the experience for students. Activities can be completed in class or as homework.

A Sample Scenario

The scenario presented in each episode is where students actually get to participate in a historical event. Let's walk through the scenario in Episode 2 to see how a simulation scenario is typically run:

After you have read or paraphrased the background for students, have each group come together in separate areas of the classroom. Describe the scene in which the British soldiers are marching toward the Village Green in Lexington. Students who are playing Patriots are standing in the green facing the advancing Redcoats. Loyalists are waiting to see how they can help the British. Undecided Citizens are watching from windows and behind stone walls to see what will happen. Each group will have a set of options to choose from as events occur. The Patriots will make their choice first. Read the following description to students playing Patriots:

Patriots, you and about 75 other minutemen have gathered on the Village Green outside Buckman Tavern. Coming toward you are several hundred Redcoats in bright red uniforms, marching in perfect order. Your commander, Captain John Parker, shouts to you: "Stand your ground; don't fire unless fired upon, but if they mean to have war, let it begin here." As you watch, a British officer comes forward and shouts, "Disperse, ye rebels, disperse!"

Now Patriots, you need to decide what to do as the British soldiers march toward you. Pick from the following choices:

1. Load your weapon and fire at the approaching soldiers.

2. Get your weapon ready and prepare to fire.

3. Duck into the tavern door to get cover in case they start shooting.

Teacher:	O.K., has everyone had enough time to decide what they want to do?
Kayla:	I am going to prepare to fire.
Teacher:	Alright. *(Noting on a piece of paper that Kayla is choosing #2)* Bob?
Bob:	Yeah, I'll do that too.
Teacher:	O.K. *(Makes a note of that)* Juan?
Juan:	That sounds good. I'll do that too.
Jennifer:	I want to do that too.
Teacher:	Alright, both Juan and Jennifer want to get their weapons ready. Mandy, you are last. What did you decide to do?
Mandy:	I'm not going to take any chances. I'm going to blast the Redcoats!
Teacher:	O.K. *(Noting all of the students' choices)* Now, let's see what happened because of your decisions. Let's start with Mandy. Mandy, you need to spin your Military Expertise number or lower in order to shoot one of the approaching Redcoats.
Mandy:	*(groaning)* I'm a lawyer. I need to spin a 2 or less!
Teacher:	Too late now. Go ahead and spin. *(Mandy spins a 5 and her Military Expertise is a 2)* As you fire at the approaching Redcoats, Captain Parker turns and yells at you, "What are you doing?" Now everyone else, spin on your Common Sense to see if you stand and fight or retreat into town as the British soldiers begin firing into your group.

This is how the scenarios will typically run, with role-playing students dealing with the situations that confront them, and you, the teacher, acting as coordinator. You present the situation in the scenario to students and then give them time to make their decisions. Do not reveal the outcome of each student's decision until everyone in the group has responded; only then do you respond to each person as the rest of the class observes and resolves the outcome of his or her choices as scripted in the scenario.

At the end of each scenario, students' Morale can be affected by how students handled the situation. For example, at the end of the above scenario, the Patriots win the Battles of Lexington and Concord and get to raise their Morale by 1, while the Loyalists subtract 1 from their Morale. The Undecided Citizens don't adjust their Morale. Next, everyone makes a Morale spin. A student must spin his Morale or lower to stay loyal to his side. If a student spins higher than her Morale, then she must make a Loyalty check and spin her Loyalty number or lower. If she spins higher than her Loyalty number, then she must move to the other side.

For example, Gina is a Loyalist with a Morale of 4. At the end of the scenario her Morale has been lowered to 3 because the Patriots have won the Battles of Lexington and Concord. She needs to spin a 3 or less to remain steadfast in her support of the king. Instead she spins a 5 and must now make a Loyalty spin. She has a Loyalty of 3 but she spins another 5. Now she is no longer a Loyalist but has moved to the Patriots. If she had made a Loyalty spin of 3 or lower then she would have remained a Loyalist. If any Undecided Citizen spins higher than her Loyalty number, then she must commit herself to either the Loyalists or the Patriots—it is her choice.

Assessing and Evaluating

Throughout the unit students should be assessed on their historical understanding. This can be done through assessing the authenticity and historical accuracy of how they play their character and the diary entries they've written throughout this simulation.

Use both rubrics on page 21 to give each student a daily score, based on the student's diary entries and your observations. Each rubric is scored on a scale of 1 to 5, with 1 being the lowest possible score and 5 the highest. Add the two scores to generate a number from 2 to 10. Convert this total score to a percentage score by multiplying it by 10. You can award scores such as 4.5 if you feel a student was at least a 4 but not quite a 5. This daily percentage score can then be averaged over the week to generate a final grade for the simulation.

	Student Log		Teacher Observations		Score Percentage
Monday	3	+	4	x 10	70%
Tuesday	4	+	4	x 10	80%
Wednesday	3.5	+	5	x 10	85%
Thursday	2.5	+	4	x 10	65%
Friday	4	+	5	x 10	90%
Average for the week					78%

For a more in-depth assessment of the students' diaries, use the rubric on page 21.

Life in the Colonies

If you lived in the colonies during the 1700s, what would you have seen? For one thing, you'd have seen people from many different countries. You might think colonists came only from Britain, but several were from Germany, the Netherlands, Ireland, and Scotland. There were also black slaves and, of course, Native Americans. Immigrants settled all along the eastern coast of the "New World." The population doubled every 25 years. The largest colony was Virginia, with New York and Massachusetts close behind.

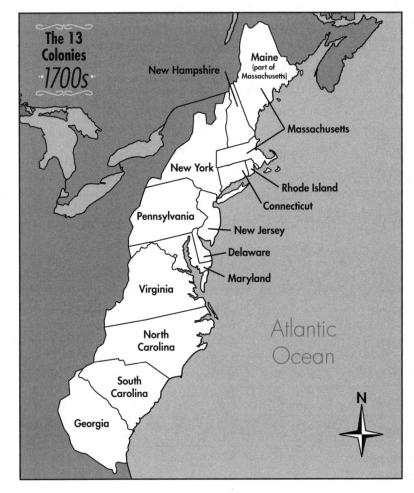

People lived in cities, villages, and farms. Most colonists worked as farmers. Others made a living as carpenters and blacksmiths, while some learned special skills like shoemaking or crafting silver. Wealthy merchants sold goods shipped in from Britain and the West Indies.

When not helping on the farm or in the family business, children would attend school. School began at 9:00 A.M. and ended at 5:00 P.M. Often classrooms contained children of

different ages. One-room schoolhouses were quite common. Books and paper were in short supply, so children had to memorize poems, stories, and verses. *The New England Primer* was the most popular textbook. In their free time, children enjoyed playing a variety of games. One popular game was "rolling the hoop." In this game, children would try to roll a wooden hoop toward a goal faster than anyone else. They also played tag, ran races, swam, fished, and played with wooden toys.

Entertainment for grown-ups came in the form of music and dance. Many dances were new to America. Musical theater was also popular. People came to hear operas in which performers sang the dialogue to tell a story. Hanging out at taverns was another form of entertainment. Here people told stories and exchanged news.

Communication in colonial times was much slower than it is today. News traveled from east to west. Newspapers, letters, and stories arrived from Britain via ships, which took about a month to reach the colonies. Once news arrived in America it spread from town to town through word of mouth. Newspapers with articles about events and life in Britain were often shared from person to person. News was also discussed in taverns and at church. Native Americans and settlers traveling west shared the news with people living in the backwoods and soldiers at forts. By the time news reached the westernmost edge of the colonies, it could be months old.

As you can imagine, travel was also slow in colonial times. Transportation was most easily done by river. Narrow, unpaved paths connected towns and villages. Most people traveled by horse, but the wealthy rode in horse-drawn carriages. It took three days to get from Philadelphia to New York City. Today it would take about two hours.

How would you have liked living in the 1700s?

Choose a Role

Select the role that you would like to play during the American Revolution simulation, then choose a name for your character. Record your choice and your attributes in your diary.

Roles	Military Expertise	Common Sense	Stamina	Negotiating Skills	Loyalty	Morale
Blacksmith	4	2	5	1	3	4
Silversmith	3	4	2	3	3	4
Indentured Servant	4	3	5	2	1	4
Tax Collector	2	3	3	3	4	4
Lawyer	2	4	1	5	3	4
Farmer	4	3	4	1	3	4
Merchant	2	5	2	4	2	4

Blacksmith – You own your own blacksmith shop. You work long hours, sometimes 10–12 hours a day. You make horseshoes for the local farmers and for the British soldiers.

Silversmith – Your expertise as a silversmith is well known in Massachusetts. The governor uses your silver during his dinner parties. In addition to making silverware, you also craft tools, buttons, watches, and jewelry.

Indentured Servant – You have been in the colonies for just over a year now. You came after a farmer paid your way. You now work for the farmer, planting and harvesting until you have paid back your debt to him. You came to the "New World" seeing an opportunity to own your own land.

Tax Collector – You have faithfully served the East India Company as an accountant for years. Recently the governor has appointed you as the tax collector for the citizens of the town.

Lawyer – You have studied law since you were 13 under a well-known lawyer in your town. Recently you decided that you have learned enough and have begun your own practice.

Farmer – The farm has been in your family for years. Your parents are buried on this land along with two of your siblings. As the firstborn son, you inherited the farm.

Merchant – Your store trades daily for the goods brought by ships sailing to and from the colonies. Your business is doing very well, as you bring in popular goods wanted by both the colonists and the British soldiers.

A Colonist's Diary

Student's Name: _____

Colonist's Name and Role: _____

_____

Colonist's Allegiance (circle one):   Loyalist   Patriot   Undecided Citizen

Colonist's Attributes:

Military Expertise: _____

Common Sense: _____

Stamina: _____

Negotiating Skills: _____

Loyalty: _____

MORALE: _____
(This number may be adjusted throughout the simulation.)

Date _____

Dear Diary,

_____

_____

_____

_____

_____

_____

_____

_____

_____

_____

_____

_____

_____

Rubric #1

Student's Diary

1 – Student did not record any events that occurred during the simulation.

2 – Student recorded very little about what occurred during the simulation.

3 – Student recorded information about what occurred during the simulation but in an incomplete fashion.

4 – Student recorded all of the important occurrences of the day's simulation, but not in a first-person narrative style.

5 – Student wrote detailed facts about the occurrences during the simulation and embellished these with personal thoughts in a believable, first-person narrative style.

Score: _____

Rubric #2

Teacher Observations

1 – Student was disruptive and prevented others from being able to participate in the simulation.

2 – Student did not participate in group discussions or simulation activities. Student might have been argumentative or disrespectful of other members of the group.

3 – Student either monopolized the group discussions or participated at a minimal level.

4 – Student participated well in the activity and allowed others to participate as well.

5 – Student was gracious in his or her participation and encouraged others to become engaged as well. Student role-played parts of the simulation to the best of his or her abilities.

Score: _____

Total score: _____

Diary Prompt Assessment Rubric

Use this rubric for a more in-depth assessment of students' diary entries.

Essential Elements	5	3	1
Historical Accuracy	Student included references to historical events consistent with the era under study. Student included descriptions and discussions of historical events that were factually accurate.	Student included references to historical events consistent with the era under study. Student provided some evidence of understanding the facts of the historical event, but included some inaccuracies or eliminated some of the most essential facts of the event.	Students did not include references to the historical event under consideration. Students provided little evidence of understanding the essential facts of the historical event under consideration.
Characterization	Student response clearly indicated that he/she assumed the role of his/her character while writing. Student response indicated how he/she felt about the events. Student demonstrated an understanding of the event and how it affected him/her as if he/she were living during that era.	Student response clearly indicated that he/she assumed the role of his/her character while writing. Student response indicated how he/she felt about the events. Student showed little evidence of understanding how the event affected his/her life.	Student response wasn't consistently written from the role of his/her character. Student responses indicated how he/she felt about the events.
Responsiveness to the Prompt	Student addressed all the essential components or questions of the diary prompt.	Student addressed most of the essential components or questions of the diary prompt.	Student response showed little relationship to the diary prompt.

Easy Simulations: American Revolution © 2007 by Renay Scott, Scholastic Teaching Resources

Simulation Spinner

DIRECTIONS:

Use this spinner at various points during the simulation to determine the outcome of a situation.

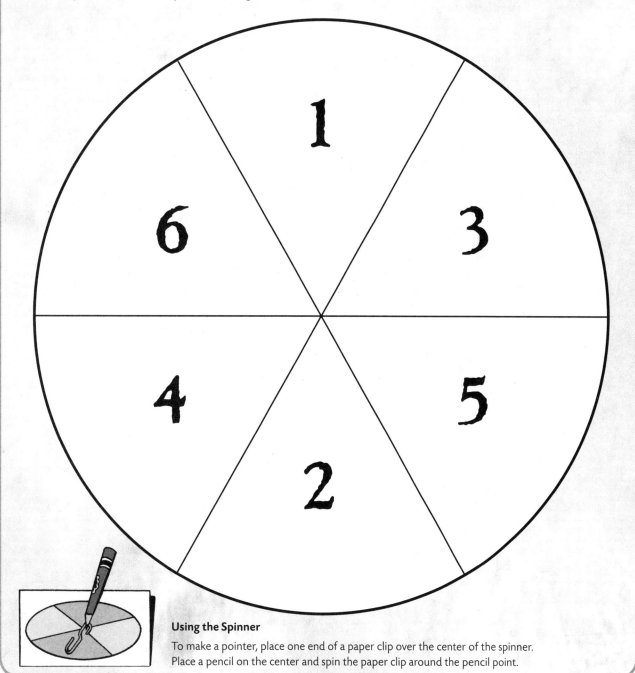

Using the Spinner

To make a pointer, place one end of a paper clip over the center of the spinner. Place a pencil on the center and spin the paper clip around the pencil point.

Episode 1

Before the Storm

OVERVIEW

Students will develop their identity through a series of activities and then introduce their characters (themselves) in a town meeting in Lexington, Massachusetts. During the town meeting, they will hear about various events happening around the colonies and then discuss their beliefs as Patriots, Loyalists, and Undecided Citizens.

ACTIVITY: WHO ARE YOU?

If you haven't done so already, divide the class into three roughly equal groups—Patriots, Loyalists, and Undecided Citizens. Invite students to choose a role, which they will assume throughout the simulation (see page 9). Students should create their own diaries (page 11) and fill out the cover page with information about their character.

Next, explain to students that in order to make their characters more believable, they will need to develop their identity as a colonist who lived in Lexington, Massachusetts, in the 1770s. First, encourage students to give their character a name. Then have them create a physical representation of their character. Physical representations can take the following forms:

- Paper doll (see page 26)

- Clay bust

- Full-size cutout

- Painting or watercolor portrait

- Sketch

If time permits, encourage students to develop their characters even further using one of the following ideas. You can also assign this activity as homework.

- Create a bio-poem (page 27)

- Create a character sketch (page 28)

SCENARIO: THE TOWN MEETING

After students have completed the character-development activities, have them introduce their character at a Lexington town meeting. Explain to students that the town meeting was the forum through which colonial citizens kept informed about the town's business and news from other colonies.

Set up the classroom to look like a meeting room. Have students bring their physical representation of their character to the meeting. Invite each student to step up to the front of the meeting and introduce him- or herself to the other citizens of Lexington. After the introductions, read aloud the following passage to inform citizens of current events:

October 17, 1774

Hear ye! Hear ye! We have gathered here at the Town Hall to discuss recent events and hear the news brought by a messenger from the colony of Pennsylvania.

First, a meeting is being held in Philadelphia. Delegates from each of the 13 colonies have been sent to Philadelphia to address the growing concerns between the colonies and King George III. These delegates, calling themselves the "Continental Congress," have selected a man by the name of Peyton Randolph to be their leader. They have agreed that each colony will have a vote, and they are working on a plan to respond to the coercive acts of the British.

In the meantime, British General Thomas Gage will be arriving in Boston, 15 miles away, with a huge armed force. He is being made civil as well as military governor.

Also, this very week, John Hancock and Joseph Warren, two of the leaders of the Sons of Liberty, are meeting in Concord to organize Patriots into minutemen militia.

Tell students: *As concerned citizens, you must be wondering how these events are going to affect you.* Have each group—the Patriots, Loyalists, and Undecided Citizens—meet in separate areas of the classroom to discuss the growing rift between the colonies and Great Britain and how this might affect their lives. Ask the Patriots to explain why they want to break away from Britain, the Loyalists to explain why it is foolish to break away from the most powerful empire on Earth, and the Undecided Citizens to discuss how they believe that there are good arguments for both sides.

Diary Prompt

Have students record what they discussed within their groups and how they feel about the events in the town meeting.

Making a Full-Body Character Paper Doll

You'll need

- large construction paper in varied skin tones
- compass
- scissors
- ruler
- glue
- pieces of fabric or colored construction paper

Gabriel Martin

To Do

1. Make the head: Use a compass to draw a 4-inch circle on a piece of construction paper. Cut out the circle.

2. Make the body: Draw a rectangle about 4 ½ inches wide by 8 inches long. Cut out the rectangle.

3. Make the arms and legs: Draw two rectangles about 4 inches long and 1 inch wide for the arms. Draw two more rectangles about 5 inches long and 1 inch wide for the legs. Cut out the rectangles for the arms and legs.

4. Construct the body: Position the head, arms, and legs on the body. Glue the pieces together on the body.

5. Make the clothing: Using the Internet and other resources, conduct research on the types of clothing worn by colonists during the colonial times. Then place the body you've constructed on a piece of fabric or colored construction paper. Trace various articles of clothing around the body to ensure a proper fit. Cut out the articles of clothing and glue them onto the figure.

6. Mount your character: To display your paper doll, glue the figure (complete with clothing) onto a piece of construction paper. Draw in the hands and shoes. Label the construction paper with your character's name.

Easy Simulations: American Revolution © 2007 by Renay Scott, Scholastic Teaching Resources

Name: _____   Date: _____

Bio-Poem

Use the following poetic style to describe yourself as a colonist. Your answers can be realistic or make-believe. Keep in mind that you will become this person throughout our unit on the American Revolution.

First name _____

Role and affiliation _____

_____   _____   _____   _____
    adjective   adjective   adjective   adjective

Who loves _____

Who felt _____

Who believed _____

Who wanted to see _____

Who gave _____

Who lives in _____

Who once said _____

Last name _____

Character Sketch Activity

A character sketch is an overview of the character's life. Use the following outline to assist you in developing your character. Then create your character sketch on a separate sheet of paper.

Step # 1: Create your character's family.

- Who was your character's father?

- Who was your character's mother?

- Did your character have any brothers or sisters?

- Where did your parents live?

- What did your parents/family do for a living?

Step # 2: Describe your birth and early childhood.

- Create a birth certificate.

Step # 3: Describe your adolescent years.

Step # 4: Describe your life now.

- Do you have a family?

- What do you currently do for a living?

- What historic events have your observed or participated in up to this point in your life?

Easy Simulations: American Revolution © 2007 by Renay Scott, Scholastic Teaching Resources

The Shot Heard Round the World

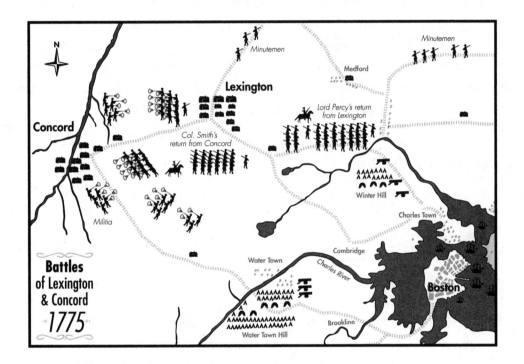

Battles of Lexington & Concord 1775

(Map labels: N, Minutemen, Minutemen, Medford, Lexington, Lord Percy's return from Lexington, Concord, Col. Smith's return from Concord, Winter Hill, Charles Town, Militia, Cambridge, Water Town, Charles River, Boston, Water Town Hill, Brookline)

OVERVIEW

Students will evaluate different primary-source accounts of the first battle of the Revolutionary War.

BACKGROUND

The Continental Congress met during the fall of 1774 to draft a petition to King George III, demanding that they be granted rights as Englishmen.

Since the Boston Massacre and the Boston Tea Party, tensions between colonial citizens and British soldiers have been high. Several colonists in Lexington and the neighboring town of Concord were storing up supplies of guns and ammunition. Loyalists in Lexington informed British General Thomas Gage about the munitions being stored.

As a result, several hundred British troops began to organize in Boston. Patriots posted lookouts to mark British movements. One lookout was silversmith Paul Revere, who was stationed on the south shore of the Charles River to watch for a signal in the Old North Church that would alert him to British troop movements. One lantern in the Old North Church would indicate that the British were coming by land, and two lanterns would mean that they were coming by sea.

On the night of April 18, 1775, Paul Revere saw two lanterns in the Old North Church. He set out on horseback to ride from town to town to warn the people that "the regulars (British soldiers) are coming out!"

Early morning on April 19, 1775, the British regiment came ashore and began their march toward Lexington. At Lexington they encountered a group of armed colonists known as minutemen. The British commander ordered the colonists to disperse when a shot rang out. Colonial and British troops exchanged gunfire. After a short exchange the British army continued its march toward Concord. Along the route they encountered light, hidden resistance by the Patriots. The events at Lexington and Concord began the War for Independence.

SCENARIO: LET IT BEGIN HERE!

Read the following accounts to students:

April 18, 1775

The British have been turning up the pressure on the colonists in Boston as well as in the surrounding towns and villages. Earlier, the Sons of Liberty had dumped hundreds of crates of expensive tea into Boston Harbor to protest the new tax on tea. Angrily, King George III ordered the arrest of the leaders of the Sons of Liberty and the capture of a rumored stash of guns and ammunition hidden in Lexington and Concord.

Only days ago, you saw Samuel Adams and John Hancock, the leaders of the Sons of Liberty, arrive in town. You know that the rumors of hidden guns and ammunition are true because you saw some of them being buried behind the tavern, with more supplies hidden in nearby Concord.

However, rumors around town say that the British are planning to move into Lexington soon to take those supplies, and you know that they are being moved to new hiding places.

April 19, 1775

Late last night word spread throughout the countryside that "the regulars (British soldiers) are coming out, the regulars are coming out!" A man you recognized as a Boston silversmith named Paul Revere went to the house of Rev. Jonas Clark, and you heard someone telling him to "stop all of that noise." You overheard Revere reply, "Noise, you'll have noise enough; the regulars are coming out!" Bells began ringing in the middle of the night and people were shouting, "To arms, to arms! The Redcoats are coming!"

Patriots who call themselves *minutemen* (because they can be ready to fight at a minute's notice) began to gather in the Buckman Tavern to hear Captain John Parker's orders and to learn about what was going on. Loyalists tried to find out how many minutemen would be gathered to fight the King's soldiers, what had happened to all of the supplies hidden by the Sons of Liberty, and if Samuel Adams and John Hancock were still in Lexington. Undecided Citizens began to gather behind stone walls and peer out of windows overlooking the Village Green, where the Patriot minutemen were gathering.

Out of the morning gloom, the sound of many marching soldiers could be heard. Soon red-uniformed British soldiers began emerging from the morning fog.

Inform students that they will be reenacting the events of the Battles of Lexington and Concord. If possible, clear an area in the middle of the room for the Village Green. Chairs and tables moved to the side can serve as "stone walls," from behind which Undecided Citizens will be waiting and watching. Have students who are Patriots stand in the Green facing the advancing Redcoats. Have students who are Loyalists stand to one side, waiting to see how they can help the British with information. As events unfold, each group will be given a set of options to choose from that will determine what happens next. Read the following passage to the Patriots, who will be the first group to decide what it will do:

Patriots, you and about 75 other minutemen have gathered on the Village Green outside Buckman Tavern. Coming toward you are several hundred Redcoats in bright red uniforms, marching in perfect order. Your commander, Captain John Parker, shouts to you: "Stand your ground; don't fire unless fired upon, but if they mean to have war, let it begin here." As you watch, a British officer comes forward and shouts, "Disperse, ye rebels, disperse!"

Now Patriots, you need to decide what to do as the British soldiers march toward you. Pick from the following choices:

1. Load your weapon and fire at the approaching soldiers.

2. Get your weapon ready and prepare to fire.

3. Duck into the tavern door to get cover in case they start shooting.

Encourage each Patriot to tell you his or her choice, making sure to take note of it on a piece of paper. After all of the Patriots have made their decision, read them the following results:

1. If you chose to fire at the approaching soldiers, make a Military Expertise spin to see how good your aim is.

   - If you spin your Military Expertise number or lower, you hit a soldier and watch as he drops his weapon and grabs his arm.

   - If you spin a number higher than your Military Expertise number, you missed.

As you fire at the approaching Redcoats, Captain Parker turns and yells at you, "What are you doing?" Now you must make a Common Sense spin to see if you stand and fight (spin your Common Sense number or lower) or retreat into town (spin a number higher than your Common Sense number) as the British soldiers begin firing into your group. If you spin a number higher than your Common Sense, then you need to make another Military Expertise spin.

   ➡ If you spin your Military Expertise number or lower, then you fire once and fall back into town as ordered by Captain Parker. Raise your Morale by 1.

➡ If you spin a number higher than your Military Expertise number, you have been wounded in the fighting and have crawled to safety. Lower your Morale by 1.

2. You prepare your weapon and wait to see what the British are going to do. Suddenly the crack of a musket being fired startles you. Who fired? You can't tell, but soon the air is filled with whining musket balls, and the man next to you clutches his chest and collapses to the ground. Captain Parker's voice can barely be heard over all of the noise but you think that you heard him yell, "Fall back!" Do you stand and fight or run back into town? If you choose to fight, then make a Military Expertise spin.

   - If you spin your Military Expertise number or lower, then you fire once and fall back into town as ordered by Captain Parker. Raise your Morale by 1.

   - If you spin a higher number than your Military Expertise, you have been wounded in the fighting and have crawled to safety. Lower your Morale by 1.

   If you decide to fall back, your Morale does not change.

3. You scramble to the door of the tavern just as you hear a shot being fired behind you. You look back to see men on both sides firing through the smoke of the muskets. You hide safely behind a table and wait this one out. Lower your Morale by 1.

Now it is the Loyalists' turn. Read these choices to the Loyalists:

Loyalists, decide what to do as the British soldiers march into the Village Green.

1. Try making it to the British officer and informing him that Samuel Adams and John Hancock fled Lexington hours ago.

2. Try telling the nearest British soldier that the Patriots have moved their supplies to new hiding places.

3. Stay put and wait this one out.

Have the Loyalists tell you what they've decided, making note of each student's choice. Then read them the following results:

1. If you chose #1, make a Negotiating Skill spin to see how well you can convince the officer that you're on his side.

    - If you spin your Negotiating Skill number or lower, you've convinced the officer that you are not a Patriot trying to trick him. Raise your Morale by 1.

    - If you spin a number higher than your Negotiating Skill, you failed, and the officer orders you arrested. Lower your Morale by 1.

2. If you chose #2, make a Common Sense spin.

    - If you spin your Common Sense number or lower, hide when the soldier aims his musket at you because he thinks that you are a Patriot attacking him.

    - If you spin a higher number, then you have been wounded and must lower your Morale by 1.

3. You watch as the British soldiers march past and on to Concord. Your Morale does not change.

Next, tell students: *The Undecided Citizens simply watch as the British march toward Concord. Later, you hear that eight minutemen were killed and 10 were wounded on the Village Green. However, by the end of the day, more than 4,000 Patriot minutemen have joined forces and attacked the British soldiers. The British suffered many casualties and had to retreat to Boston with the Patriots hard on their heels. It is a great victory for the Patriots in the first battle of the American Revolution. All of the Loyalists must lower their Morale by 1. All of the Patriots raise their Morale by 1.*

Now, have all students make a Morale spin to see how they feel about their allegiance. Students who spin their Morale number or lower feel good about where they stand, whether it be Patriot, Loyalist, or Undecided Citizens. If students spin a number higher than their Morale number, then they must also make a Loyalty spin. If they spin their Loyalty number or less, they stay on their side. If they spin a higher number, then they switch sides.

DIARY PROMPT

Have students write a diary entry about today's dramatic events. Remind them to write in character.

ACTIVITY: WHODUNNIT?

Students will evaluate different primary sources to see which account is the most reliable. Before starting the activity, assemble an "Investigation Packet" for every group of four students in your class.

Making an Investigation Packet

YOU'LL NEED

- yellow 10-by-12-inch mailing envelope

- 6 Primary Source documents (pages 37–42)

- 5 copies of Credibility of Witness Form (page 43)

To Do

In the mailing envelope, put a copy of each of the six primary source documents at the end of this section. Also, put in a copy of the Credibility of Witness form for each student in the group, plus one extra for the group's final copy.

Inform your class that today is August 20, 1775, and they have been summoned to the Lexington Green. Once assembled, tell the colonists that you have received a letter from General Joseph Palmer about the events of April 19, 1775. Assign a "town crier" to read the letter to the citizens of Lexington:

Primary Source Document

Letter from Joseph Palmer

Wednesday morning near 10 of the clock – Watertown. To all friends of American liberty, be it known that this morning before break of day, a brigade, consisting of about 1,000 to 1,200 men, landed at Phip's farm at Cambridge and marched to Lexington, where they found a company of our colony militia in arms, upon whom they fired without any provocation and killed six and wounded four others. By an express from Boston, we find another brigade are now upon their march from Boston supposed to be about 1,000. The Bearer, Israel Bissell, is charged to alarm the country quite to Connecticut and all persons are desired to furnish him with fresh horses as they may be needed. I have spoken with several persons who have seen the dead and wounded. Pray let the delegates from this colony to Connecticut see this.

J. Palmer, one of the Committee of Safety.

Inform the citizens of Lexington that the other colonies are very concerned about the events of April 19th and desire to know what actually happened at Lexington and Concord. Students will need to investigate the events and write a report to the Committee of Correspondence and to the newspaper *The Lexington Times*. Explain to students that each town had a Committee of Correspondence, which was responsible for spreading information about important events that occurred in the colonies. Any important event that happened in one town was recorded in a letter and given to a colonial, who road by horseback throughout the area, announcing the news.

For this investigation, divide the citizens of Lexington into small groups of four. Make sure that members of each group share the same affiliation (Patriots, Loyalists, or Undecided Citizens). Give each group an "Investigation Packet" and assign roles to each group member, as follows:

- **Recorder:** Records the group's final consensus about the witness's credibility on a Credibility of Witnesses form. Also keeps time and moves the group discussion along to ensure that the task is completed by the end of the allotted time.

- **Reporter:** Reports the group's final decision to the citizens of Lexington at a town meeting to discuss the events. Also facilitates the group's discussion of sources.

- **Reader 1:** Reads three primary source documents to the group.

- **Reader 2:** Reads three primary source documents to the group.

Instruct students to listen carefully to the documents as they are read within their groups and to make notes about the various documents. After all of the documents have been read, each member of the group should determine how credible (believable) the documents are and rate each document on his or her own Credibility of Witness form. After each group member has filled out his or her form, the group should discuss each document and arrive at a consensus about each document's credibility.

When all the groups are finished, call another town meeting and invite the reporter from each group to share his or her group's rankings with the entire town. Other citizens will be given an opportunity to question each group about its rankings and the order of credibility.

After the town meeting, tell students that each group should prepare a report to the Committee of Correspondence, recounting what it believes happened on April 19, 1775. The report should include an explanation of who fired the first shot. Explain to the class that historical accounts are often written from a perspective, and perspective often depends on a person's relationship to the events. Tell students that when they write their report to the Committee, they should write from their perspective as Patriots, Loyalists, or Undecided Citizens. Also, inform students that their character will assume this perspective for the remainder of the simulation.

DOCUMENT 1

Lieutenant John Barker

British Officer

(DIARY ENTRY WRITTEN ON APRIL 19, 1775)

19th. At 2 'oclock we began our March by wading through a very long ford up to our Middles: after going a few miles we took 3 or 4 People who were going off to give intelligence; about 5 miles on this side of a Town called Lexington which lay in our road, we heard there were some hundreds of People collected together intending to oppose us and stop our going on; at 5 'oclock we arrived there, and saw a number of People, I believe between 2 and 300, formed on a Common in the middle of the Town; we still continued advancing, keeping prepared against an attack tho' without intending to attack them, but on our coming near them they fired one or two shots, upon which our Men without any orders rushed in upon them, fired and put 'em to flight; several of them were killed, we cou'd not tell how many, because they were got behind Walls and into the Woods; We had a Man of the 10th light Infantry wounded, nobody else hurt. We then formed on the Common but with some difficulty, the Men were so wild they cou'd hear no orders; we waited a considerable time there and at length proceeded on our way to Concord, which we then learnt was our destination, in order to destroy a Magazine of stores collected there.

DOCUMENT 2

Jeremy Lister

British Officer at Lexington

(PERSONAL NARRATIVE WRITTEN IN 1782)

To the best of my recollection about 4 o'clock in the morning being the 19th of April the front companies was ordered to load which we did . . . It was at Lexington when we saw one of their Compys (companies) drawn up in regular order. Major Pitcairn of the Marines second in Command call'd to them to disperse, but their not seeming willing he desired us to mind our space which we did when they gave us a fire then runoff to get behind a wall. We had one man wounded of our Compy in the leg, his name was Johnson, also Major Pitcairn's Horse was shot in the flank; we returned their salute, and before we proceeded on our march from Lexington I believe we kill'd and wounded either 7 or 8 men.

DOCUMENT 3

Joseph Warren

President pro tem of the
Massachusetts Provincial Congress

(IN A COVER LETTER FOR 21 SWORN DEPOSITIONS ABOUT
THE EVENTS AT LEXINGTON AND CONCORD SENT TO BENJAMIN FRANKLIN,
THE COLONIAL REPRESENTATIVE IN LONDON)

To the Inhabitants of Great Britain: In Provincial Congress, Watertown, April 26, 1775.

Friends and Fellow Subjects: Hostilities are at length commenced in the Colony by the troops under command of General Gage; and it being of the greatest importance that an early, true and authentic account of this inhuman proceeding should be known to you, the Congress of this Colony have transmitted the same, and from want of a session of the honorable Continental Congress, think it proper to address you on the alarming occasion.

By the clearest depositions relative to the transaction, it will appear that on the night preceding the nineteenth of April instant . . . the Town of Lexington . . . was alarmed, and a colony of the inhabitants mustered on the occasion; that the Regular troops, on their way to Concord, marched into the said town of Lexington, and the said company, on their approach, began to disperse; that notwithstanding this, the regular rushed on with great violence, and first began hostilities by firing on said Lexington Company, whereby they killed eight and wounded several others; that the Regulars continued their fire until those of said company, who were neither killed nor wounded, had made their escape.

These brethren are marks of ministerial vengeance against this colony, for refusing, with her sister colonies, a submission to slavery. But they have not yet detached us from our Royal Sovereign. We profess to be his loyal and dutiful subjects, and so hardly dealt with as we have been, are still ready, with our lives and fortunes, to defend his person, family, crown and destiny. Nevertheless, to the persecution and tyranny of his cruel ministry we will not tamely submit; appealing to Heaven for the justice of our cause, we determine to die or to be free.

DOCUMENT 4

Nathaniel Mulliken, Phillip Russell,

and 32 other men duly sworn to be 34 minutemen

on April 25th, 1775, before three Justices of the Peace

We Nathaniel Mulliken, Philip Russell, (and 32 others who are named) . . . all of lawful age, and inhabitants of Lexington, in the Country of Middlesex, . . . do testify and declare, that on the nineteenth of April instant, about one or two o'clock in the morning, being informed that . . . a body of regulars were marching from Boston towards Concord, . . . we were alarmed and having met at the place of our company's parade (Lexington Green), were dismissed by our Captain, John Parker, for the present, with orders to be ready to attend at the beat of the drum. We further testify and declare that about five o'clock in the morning, hearing our drum beat, we proceeded towards the parade, and soon found that a large body of troops were marching towards us, some of our company were coming to the parade, and others had reached it, at which time the company began to disperse, whilst our backs were turned on the troops, we were fired on by them, and a number of our men were instantly killed and wounded, not a gun was fired by any person in our company on the regulars to our knowledge before they fired on us, and they continued firing until we had all made our escape.

Easy Simulations: American Revolution © 2007 by Renay Scott, Scholastic Teaching Resources

DOCUMENT 5

NEWSPAPER ACCOUNT

THE LONDON GAZETTE

JUNE 10, 1775

Lieutenant Nunn, of the Navy arrived this morning at Lord Darthmouth's and brought letters from General Gage, Lord Percy, and Lieutenant-Colonel Smith, containing the following particulars of what passed on the nineteenth of April last between a detachment of the King's Troops in the Province of Massachusetts-Bay and several parties of rebel provincials . . . Lieutenant-Colonel Smith finding, after he had advanced some miles on his march, that the country had been alarmed by the firing of guns and ringing of bells, dispatched six companies of light-infantry, in order to secure two bridges on different roads beyond Concord, who, upon their arrival at Lexington, found a body of the country people under arms, on a green close to the road; and upon the King's Troops marching up to them, in order to inquire the reason of their being so assembled, they went off in great confusion, and several guns were fired upon the King's troops from behind a stone wall, and also from the meeting-house and other houses, by which one man was wounded, and Major Pitcairn's horse shot in two places. In consequence of this attack by the rebels, the troops returned the fire and killed several of them. After which the detachment marched on to Concord without any thing further happening.

DOCUMENT 6

TRANSCRIBED FROM *THE UNITED STATES: STORY OF A FREE PEOPLE* (PUBLISHED BY ALLYN AND BACON IN 1963)

In April 1775, General Gage, the military governor of Massachusetts, sent out a body of troops to take possession of military stores at Concord, a short distance from Boston. At Lexington, a handful of "embattled farmers," who had been tipped off by Paul Revere, barred the way. The "rebels" were ordered to disperse. They stood their ground. The English fired a volley of shots that killed eight patriots. It was not long before the swift-riding Paul Revere spread the news of this new atrocity to the neighboring colonies. The patriots of all New England, although still a handful, were now to fight the English.

Name: _____   Date: _____

Credibility of Witness Form

After listening to all the primary source documents, complete this form individually. Rank each document's credibility, from 1 (for least credible) to 5 (for most credible). Once each member of your group has completed the form, talk about your individual rankings and come up with one set of rankings that represents your group's consensus. Complete a separate Credibility of Witnesses form for your group.

```
      1           2           3           4           5
      |           |           |           |           |
least credible                                  most credible
```

Witnesses	Your Ranking	Reasons for Your Ranking
John Barker		
Jeremy Lister		
Joseph Warren		
Nathaniel Mulliken, Phillip Russell, and 32 other minutemen		
The London Gazette		
The United States: Story of a Free People		

Declaring Independence

OVERVIEW

After reading the Declaration of Independence, Patriots and Loyalists will brainstorm ways to recruit the Undecided Citizens over to their side. Meanwhile, Undecided Citizens will compile a list of pros and cons for joining each of the other groups. Then colonists will make a spin to determine their loyalty.

BACKGROUND

The events of April 19, 1775, marked the beginning of what historians call the War for Independence. The colonists felt that the British government did not take their needs into consideration when creating laws for the colonies. The British government claimed that the colonies were the property of Britain, and as such, must obey their laws. On July 4, 1776, the Continental Congress voted to adopt the Declaration of Independence, which detailed the reasons why the colonies were breaking away from Britain. In Philadelphia the Declaration of Independence was read aloud at Carpenter's Hall for all to hear. Soon

copies of the Declaration were spreading throughout the colonies and being read in the cities, towns, and villages of America.

ACTIVITY: READING THE DECLARATION OF INDEPENDENCE

Students will read sections of the Declaration of Independence and discuss what the document means and how it affects their lives as colonists. The entire Declaration will not be read, and you may have to help interpret some of the language for students. This experience will provide some valuable insight into why the Patriots wanted to form their own nation.

YOU'LL NEED

- Section 1 of the Declaration of Independence (page 47)

- Section 2 of the Declaration of Independence (page 48)

- Section 3 of the Declaration of Independence (page 49)

To Do

Make enough photocopies of each section of the Declaration of Independence so that all students in each group will have their own copy. Section 1 will go to the Patriots, Section 2 to the Undecided Citizens, and Section 3 to the Loyalists.

Assemble the citizens of Lexington to listen to the reading of the Declaration of Independence. Have the Patriots, Undecided Citizens, and Loyalists sit with their own groups. Hand each group a section of the Declaration. Inform them that the reading of the Declaration of Independence was a monumental event in history. Assign a representative from each group to read aloud their section of the Declaration, then invite members of the group to comment on what they think that section means and how it might affect their particular group.

Next, have each group move to separate areas of the classroom—the Patriots should "set up camp" on one side of the room and the Loyalists on the opposite side. Place the Undecided Citizens between the two sides. Instruct the Patriots and Loyalists to conduct research and find out why each side believed it was right in fighting for their independence or staying loyal to the British crown (see Resources, page 62). Each group should brainstorm and make a list of reasons why the Undecided Citizens should join its side.

At the same time, tell Undecided Citizens to conduct research on the various people living in the colonies—women, Native Americans, foreign visitors, African-Americans—and how the Declaration of Independence and the coming war might affect them. Have them brainstorm pros and cons for joining the Patriots or the Loyalists and create a list of these pros and cons.

After students have completed their lists, invite each group to share them with the rest of the class. Discuss each group's reasons for joining the Patriots or Loyalists, as well as the Undecided Citizens' list of pros and cons.

SCENARIO: WE WANT YOU!

Loyalists and Patriots throughout the colonies tried to convince Undecided Citizens to join their cause. In this scenario, each Patriot and each Loyalist will pick an Undecided Citizen to persuade to join their group. Each Patriot and Loyalist will get only one chance.

Patriots and Loyalists take turns, with the Loyalists going first. Pick a Loyalist and ask her to choose an Undecided Citizen whom she wants to join the Loyalist cause. The Loyalist must first give the Citizen a reason to support the king, and then make a Negotiating Skill spin.

- If she spins her own Negotiating Skill number or lower, then she has convinced the Undecided Citizen to become a Loyalist.

- If she spins a number higher than her Negotiating Skill, the Loyalist has failed and the Citizen remains undecided.

Next, pick a Patriot to do the same thing. An Undecided Citizen can be picked more than once, as long as he or she still belongs to the Undecided group. This back-and-forth picking will continue until all of the Patriots and Loyalists have had a chance to try to persuade an Undecided Citizen to commit to their side.

DIARY PROMPT

Have students write in their diaries about how the Declaration will affect their decision to be Patriots, Loyalists, or Undecided Citizens. To help them elaborate on their diary entry, you may want to use the following prompts for each group:

Patriots: Write how you feel about being a Patriot. Are you excited? Are you scared? Why do you feel that you should fight for your independence?

Loyalist: Write how you feel about being a Loyalist. Are you scared? Do you feel outnumbered? How can you contribute to the cause of defeating the rebellion?

Undecided Citizens: How do you feel about the War for Independence? Who do you think might win the war? How will your life change if the group you think will win the war actually wins the war?

The Declaration of Independence

(SECTION 1)

When in the Course of human events, it becomes necessary for one people to dissolve the political bands which have connected them with another, and to assume among the powers of the earth, the separate and equal station to which the Laws of Nature and of Nature's God entitle them, a decent respect to the opinions of mankind requires that they should declare the causes which impel them to the separation.

The Declaration of Independence

(SECTION 2)

We hold these truths to be self-evident, that all men are created equal, that they are endowed by their Creator with certain unalienable Rights, that among these are Life, Liberty and the pursuit of Happiness. —That to secure these rights, Governments are instituted among Men, deriving their just powers from the consent of the governed, —That whenever any Form of Government becomes destructive of these ends, it is the Right of the People to alter or to abolish it, and to institute new Government, laying its foundation on such principles and organizing its powers in such form, as to them shall seem most likely to effect their Safety and Happiness.

Easy Simulations: American Revolution © 2007 by Renay Scott, Scholastic Teaching Resources

The Declaration of Independence

(SECTION 3)

Prudence, indeed, will dictate that Governments long established should not be changed for light and transient causes; and accordingly all experience hath shewn that mankind are more disposed to suffer, while evils are sufferable than to right themselves by abolishing the forms to which they are accustomed. But when a long train of abuses and usurpations, pursuing invariably the same Object evinces a design to reduce them under absolute Despotism, it is their right, it is their duty, to throw off such Government, and to provide new Guards for their future security. . . .

The history of the present King of Great Britain is a history of repeated injuries and usurpations, all having in direct object the establishment of an absolute Tyranny over these States. . . . In every stage of these Oppressions We have Petitioned for Redress in the most humble terms: Our repeated Petitions have been answered only by repeated injury. A Prince, whose character is thus marked by every act which may define a Tyrant, is unfit to be the ruler of a free people.

Winter at Valley Forge

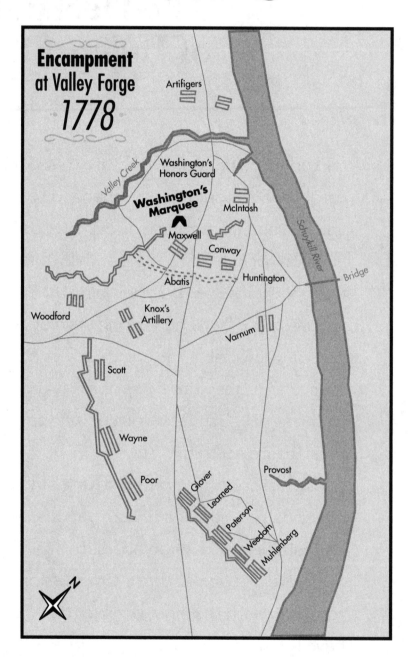

Encampment at Valley Forge 1778

Artifigers

Valley Creek

Washington's Honors Guard

Washington's Marquee

McIntosh

Maxwell

Conway

Schuylkill River

Abatis

Huntington

Bridge

Woodford

Knox's Artillery

Varnum

Scott

Wayne

Poor

Glover

Learned

Provost

Paterson

Weedom

Muhlenberg

OVERVIEW

Students compare the lifestyles of soldiers in the Continental (American) army and the British army during the winter of 1777–1778.

BACKGROUND

Valley Forge was an encampment for the Continental army during the winter of 1777–1778. While the Continental army camped out in Valley Forge, British forces stayed in the city of Philadelphia for the winter. Accounts of the weather that winter identified two periods of severe cold—the end of December and the end of March. Three snowstorms, best described as continuous and steady rather than blizzard-like, also hit the area. In February the heavy snowfall was followed by heavy rain, making roads muddy and impassable. The winter also included several periods of above-normal temperatures.

Such conditions may not have been so bad if the Continental army had been well supplied. But quartermasters and commissary generals, who were responsible for issuing supplies to the army, resigned around mid-1777. Remaining commissary agents were not always efficient and attentive to their duties, and soldiers were left without food and supplies. Exacerbating the problem was the decline in colonial currency, making private trade more attractive. Consequently, farmers and merchants were reluctant to sell their goods to commissary agents.

Surprisingly, these challenges toughened the 6,000 Continental soldiers who remained with General George Washington at Valley Forge. In some respects, the winter at Valley Forge could be considered a turning point in the Revolutionary War. Valley Forge symbolizes patriotism with the suffering, courage, and perseverance of the men who encamped that winter.

ACTIVITY: THE WAR GOES ON

At this point, most of the Undecided Citizens should have already decided which side they are going to join. If you still have Undecided Citizens, have each of those Citizens choose which side he wants to join and then spin his Loyalty number or lower to join his chosen side. If a Citizen spins a number higher than his Loyalty number, then he must join the other side.

Now that all students are either Patriots or Loyalists, each group must set up camp on opposite sides of the room and design the uniforms and flags that will represent their regiment.

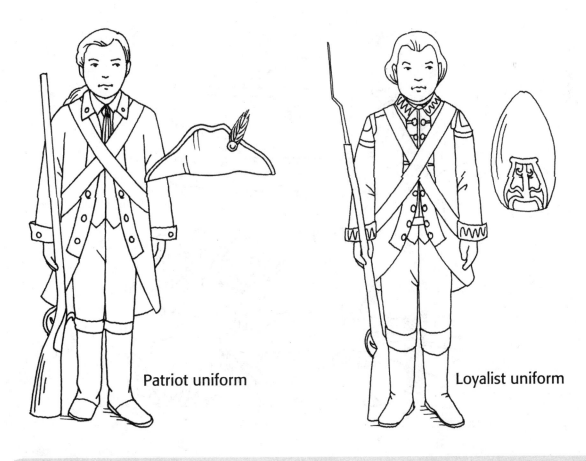

Patriot uniform

Loyalist uniform

Have students conduct research on the uniforms and flags that were used by both sides during the Revolutionary War (see Resources, page 62). Also, each group should decide on a name for its regiment. The names should also reflect ones used during the war.

Have each group present its regiment name, uniform, and flag to the class and explain the reasoning behind its choices.

SCENARIO: THE WORST AND BEST OF TIMES

Tell students that in this scenario, they are going to be either Patriots camped out at Valley Forge or Loyalists stationed in Philadelphia. Inform students that after General George Washington's defeat at the Battle of Brandywine, the British captured the city of Philadelphia, and General Washington was forced to take his army and spend the winter 25 miles west, at Valley Forge. The Continental army stayed there from December 19, 1777 until June 19, 1778. When it arrived at Valley Forge, the army numbered around 11,000 men, but by the end of winter only about 6,000 men were left. Around 2,500 men had died from starvation, cold, and disease. Another 2,500 had deserted the army and gone home. Read aloud the following diary account from Albigence Waldo, a surgeon at Valley Forge in 1777, to give students an idea of what the Patriot soldiers experienced that winter.

December 21

[Valley Forge.] Preparations are made for huts. Provisions Scarce. Mr. Ellis went homeward – sent a Letter to my Wife. Heartily wish myself at home, my Skin and eyes are almost spoil'd with continual smoke. A general cry thro' the Camp this Evening among the Soldiers, "No Meat! No Meat!" – the Distant vales Echo'd back the melancholy sound – "No Meat! No Meat!" Immitating the noise of Crows and Owls, also, made a part of confused Musick. "What have you for your dinner boys?" "Nothing but Fire Cake and Water, Sir." At night, "Gentlemen the Supper is ready." What is your Supper Lads? "Fire Cake and Water, Sir." Very poor beef has been drawn in our Camp the greater part of this season. A Butcher bringing a Quarter of this kind of Beef into Camp one day who had white Buttons on the knees of his breeches, a Soldier cries out – "There, there Tom is some more of your fat Beef, by my soul I can see the Butcher's breeches buttons through it."

It was a desperate time for General Washington and the rest of the Patriots, but the 6,000 that remained were turned into one of the best fighting forces on the continent, with the help of Prussian officer Baron Von Steuben. Read the following to the Patriots group:

January 5, 1778

Patriots, you have lost Philadelphia, one of the most important cities in the colonies, to the Redcoats. You are tired and hungry, and it has started to snow again. Your shoes wore out last November, and you have not been able to replace them. You wrap torn cloth around your feet and wince as you leave bloody footprints in the snow from your cracked and bleeding feet. Three days ago you watched one of your best friends die from a fever and hunger. What are you going to do? Choose from one of the following:

1. Try making shoes and clothing out of material that you can scrounge up from around camp.

2. Try to build a better hut for shelter against the cold and snow.

3. Go out and try foraging for food in the woods.

Ask each Patriot to tell you his or her choice, making sure to take note of it on a piece of paper. After all of the Patriots have made their decision, read them the following results:

1. If you chose #1, spin your Common Sense number or lower to make better clothes and shoes for yourself.

   • If you spin a number higher than your Common Sense number, your Morale goes down by one point.

   • If you succeed on your Common Sense spin, add one point to your Stamina. Next, spin your Stamina number or lower. If you succeed, your Morale stays the same. If you spin a higher number than your Stamina, your Morale goes down by one.

2. If you chose to try to build a better hut, spin your Military Expertise number or lower to see if you remember how to build an army hut for shelter.

   • If you spin a number higher than your Military Expertise number, your Morale goes down by one point.

   • If you succeed on your Military Expertise spin, add one point to your Stamina. Next, spin your Stamina number or lower. If you succeed, your Morale stays the same. If you spin a higher number than your Stamina, your Morale goes down by one.

3. If you decided to go foraging for food, spin your Stamina number or lower to be able to endure the cold long enough to find some food.

   • If you spin a number higher than your Stamina number, your Morale goes down by one point.

   • If you succeed, raise your Stamina by one point. Spin your Stamina number or lower again. If you succeed, then your Morale stays the same. If you spin a higher number than your Stamina, your Morale goes down by one.

Next, have each Patriot make another Morale spin:

   • If a Patriot spins her Morale number or lower, she decides to tough it out with General Washington at Valley Forge.

   • If a Patriot spins a number higher than his Morale, then he must make a Loyalty spin. If the Patriot spins a number equal to or lower than his Loyalty number, then he stays with General Washington. If the number is higher than his Loyalty number, then that Patriot has deserted the army and joined the Loyalists.

Now, read the following to the Loyalists staying in Philadelphia:

January 5, 1778

Loyalists, you are enjoying the warmth and party atmosphere of Philadelphia during the winter of 1777–78. Choose one of the following:

1. Accept an invitation from General Charles Cornwallis to a formal ball. Raise your Morale by one point.

2. Go shopping for some better clothes and a nice beaver hat to keep your ears warm. Raise your Morale by one point.

3. Read the news about how the rebels are either being defeated or in hiding all through the colonies. Raise your Morale by one point.

Inform the Loyalists that British soldiers made fun of the Patriots by making up a song called "Yankee Doodle." Have the Loyalists sing the following verses of the song:

Yankee Doodle came to town
For to buy a firelock
We will tar and feather him
And so we will John Hancock

Yankee Doodle keep it up
Yankee Doodle Dandy
Mind the music and the step
And with the girls be handy

By now, students should realize that the war was going quite well for the British at this point. That is why all of the Loyalists get to raise their Morale. The party atmosphere in Philadelphia at that time showed that the British did not take the threat of Washington's army only 25 miles away very seriously.

DIARY PROMPT

Have Patriots write in their diaries about their life at Valley Forge, elaborating on the weather, their hardships, and their activities there. Encourage them to use information from their research and the simulation to help formulate their diary entry.

Similarly, have Loyalists write about their life in Philadelphia and how they think the war is going for them.

Yorktown

OVERVIEW

Students learn about the triumphs and defeats of both sides of the Revolutionary War and experience an actual battle in Yorktown.

BACKGROUND

The winter at Valley Forge had molded a ragtag volunteer army into a seasoned, disciplined force, with the help of Baron Von Steuben, a Prussian officer enlisted by General George Washington. An alliance with France, coupled with the French navy sailing toward the North American shores caused the British army to reassess its location in Philadelphia.

In June of 1778, the British army left Philadelphia under the new command of General Sir Henry Clinton and set out for Manhattan. Hot weather and heavy rains slowed the British march. The Continental army soon overtook the British soldiers and engaged them in battle at Monmouth Court House, New Jersey. The battle was a draw, and under the cover of night the British withdrew and reached Manhattan.

Making little progress in the North, the British decided to take the war to the southern colonies, where they believed they would find more support from the Loyalists. In late 1778, the British captured the major port city of Savannah, Georgia. Shortly after, they also took the city of Augusta. In February 1780, General Charles Cornwallis took the critical port city of Charleston, South Carolina. Here, the British captured 5,000 soldiers and numerous supplies, wiping out most of the southern Continental army. With such success in the South, Clinton left Cornwallis in charge of the southern army and returned his troops to New York. Cornwallis continued to lay claim to the colonial territory, beginning in the South and moving toward the North.

The Continental Congress then sent General Horatio Gates to disrupt the British activities in the South. As Gates marched to Camden, South Carolina, he lost many men in the wilderness and swamp lands. Once at Camden, in the face of the British army, the colonials turned and ran. This marked a new low point for the Continental army. In September 1780 the Continental army suffered another blow when it was discovered that General Benedict Arnold had turned traitor. The British proceeded with great confidence through the South, attempting to systematically wipe out the Continental army.

The Continental army decided upon a risky strategy to counteract the British success. Colonial Major General Nathanael Greene, commander of the southern army, split his troops and sent a small force west while the remainder of his force camped near the South Carolina border under Brigadier General Daniel Morgan. Cornwallis sent a force to meet Morgan. They met at Cowpens, a cattle-grazing field in South Carolina. The battle was a disaster for the British. Cornwallis angrily chased Greene, who had joined Morgan, through North Carolina and into Virginia. The chase took its toll on the British army. Along the way British soldiers burned and abandoned their supplies in an attempt to become lighter and faster. Still, they could not catch Greene. Finally, at Guilford's Courthouse, the two forces met. The battle was intense. The British victory came at a heavy cost. Twice as many British soldiers as Continental soldiers were lost. Cornwallis ordered his army to withdraw to Wilmington, North Carolina.

While these battles raged in the South, little fighting was taking place in the North. General Washington employed the assistance of the French navy, which sailed around New York, cutting off a British withdrawal by water. Washington then headed for Virginia, planning to trap Cornwallis by land at Yorktown, while the French navy stationed at Chesapeake Bay blocked any chance of the British army's escape by sea. Cornwallis knew his chances of defeating the Continental army were slim.

The Continental army and French navy bombarded the town. British supplies inside Yorktown were running short. With no chance of reinforcements, Cornwallis decided to surrender.

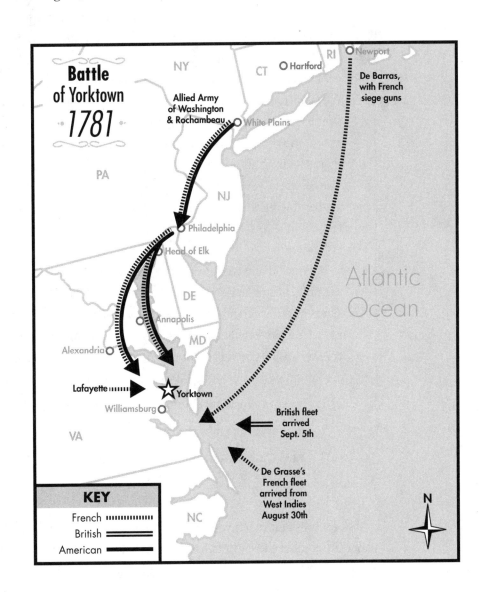

SCENARIO: THE END IS NEAR

After sharing the above history with students, explain that in this scenario the Patriots will be assaulting the defenses surrounding the British position at Yorktown. The Loyalists will be defending Yorktown from the Patriots. At this point, there should no longer be any Undecided Citizens—every student should have cast his or her lot with either the Patriots or the Loyalists.

Read the following to the Patriots group:

October 17, 1781

Patriots, you can smell the ocean nearby and glimpse the French flags flying from the masts of the French fleet under the command of Admiral Francois Joseph De Grasse. As the first light of day dawns you hear the thunder of the French ships' cannons firing on the defenses of Yorktown once again. You flinch as the cannons of the Continental and French armies surrounding Yorktown join in with the French fleet to pound the British-held city. This siege has lasted for more than two weeks now, and with every passing day the defenses of Yorktown get weaker and weaker.

You snap to attention as you hear the booming German-accented voice of Baron Von Steuben, your commanding officer and the man who taught you how to be a soldier during that hard winter in Yorktown. He orders your company into marching formation—you will try to dislodge the British soldiers from their positions outside of Yorktown.

You set off at a run toward the dirt embankments hiding the British soldiers and see puffs of smoke rising from their cannons. The ground shakes as a cannon ball slams into the earth behind you. Now you see many smaller clouds of smoke as the British musketeers begin to fire at your soldiers. Yet there are not nearly as many enemy muskets firing at you now as there were two weeks ago. You approach the embankment and begin to charge up the dirt slope. Now choose from the following:

1. Fire your musket and jump over the embankment.

2. Jump over the embankment and fire at the first enemy soldier.

3. Crawl carefully over the embankment.

Ask each Patriot to tell you his or her choice, making sure to take note of it on a piece of paper. After all of the Patriots have made their decision, read them the following results:

1. If you chose #1, your fire made the enemy soldier duck down, and as you jump over the embankment you land on top of him and knock him senseless.

2. You jump over the embankment and see a musket pointed at you. Make a Military Expertise spin to see if you shoot him before he shoots you.

- If you spin your Military Expertise number or lower, you have fired first, and you watch the Redcoat collapse to the ground.

- If you spin a number higher than your Military Expertise number, the enemy has shot you, and you collapse with a musket ball in your leg.

3. By the time you get over the embankment, your fellow soldiers have already routed the enemy, and you watch as they retreat to Yorktown.

Now read the following to the Loyalists:

October 17, 1781

Loyalists, you wake to the thunder of the French naval guns and hunker down behind the embankment. You know that the cannons of General George Washington and French General Comte Jean-Baptiste de Rochambeau will soon be bombarding your position just outside of Yorktown. You try not to think about your empty stomach and nearly empty ammunition pouch as the Continental army's guns begin pounding the ground around you.

You have heard rumors that General Charles Cornwallis is considering surrendering because the French fleet has cut off any chance of getting reinforcements by sea, and with the Continental and French armies cutting off all of the land routes, it's impossible to escape. This is unbelievable! How could the greatest nation on Earth, with the best-trained and -equipped army in the world, be losing to a bunch of shopkeepers and farmers?

You peek over the embankment when you hear your own cannons firing. The Patriot soldiers must be attacking again. You fire your musket into the mass of charging soldiers and try to reload, only to feel the bottom of your ammunition pouch. As the enemy starts charging up the dirt embankment with their sharp bayonets pointed toward you, think about what you will do next. Choose from the following:

1. Fix your bayonet on your musket and prepare to meet the charge.

2. Try moving to where there are more British or Loyalist soldiers, to get more ammunition.

3. Jump from the embankment and make your way back to Yorktown.

Ask each Loyalist to tell you his or her choice, making sure to take note of it on a piece of paper. After all of the Patriots have made their decision, read them the following results:

1. If you chose #1, a Patriot soldier jumps over the embankment and aims his musket at you. Spin your Military Expertise number or lower to stab him with your bayonet before he can shoot you.

   - If you succeed he goes down, but you see that it is hopeless to stay when more and more Patriots pour over the embankment. You retreat to Yorktown.

   - If you spin a number higher than your Military Expertise number, then the soldier blocks your thrust and fires, the ball grazes your head, and you fall unconscious to the earth.

2. As you begin moving toward your fellow soldiers you find yourself surrounded by musket-carrying Patriots. A Patriot officer points his sword at you and demands your surrender. Having no choice, you drop your musket and raise your hands.

3. As you run back to Yorktown, you glance behind and see that the Patriots have taken over the embankments that you have just abandoned.

ACTIVITY: SURRENDER AT YORKTOWN

Read aloud the following entries from the diary of Ebenezer Denny, a major in the Continental army, relating the capture of General Cornwallis at Yorktown in 1781.

Primary Source Document

October 17th.-

In the morning, before relief came, had the pleasure of seeing a drummer mount the enemy's parapet, and beat a parley, and immediately an officer, holding up a white handkerchief, made his appearance outside their works; the drummer accompanied him, beating. Our batteries ceased. An officer from our lines ran and met the other, and tied the handkerchief over his eyes. The drummer sent back, and the British officer conducted to a house in rear of our lines. Firing ceased totally.

18th.-

Several flags pass and repass now even without the drum. Had we not seen the drummer in his red coat when he first mounted, he might have beat away till doomsday. The constant firing was too much for the sound of a single drum; but when the firing ceased, I thought I never heard a drum equal to it—the most delightful music to us all.

(Continued)

19th.-

Our division man the lines again. All is quiet. Articles of capitulation signed; detachments of French and Americans take possession of British forts. Major Hamilton commanded a battalion which took possession of a fort immediately opposite our right and on the bank of York river. I carried the standard of our regiment on this occasion. On entering the fort, Baron Steuben, who accompanied us, took the standard from me and planted it himself. The British army parade and march out with their colors furled; drums beat as if they did not care how. Grounded their arms and returned to town. . . . Lord Cornwallis excused himself from marching out with the troops; they were conducted by General O'Hara.

Clear a large area in your classroom in which you can reenact the British surrender at Yorktown. Have the Patriots line up shoulder to shoulder, silently awaiting the British soldiers to march in and face them. Have Loyalists march into the classroom holding a white flag. Keep in mind that General Cornwallis did not attend this surrender. Once the Loyalist soldiers have marched in, they should throw down their weapons in a pile.

Now the Patriot soldiers sing their own version of "Yankee Doodle." Tell students that the Continental army took the song that the British had used to mock the colonists and turned it into a patriotic song that they sang with pride:

Father and I went down to camp
Along with Captain Goodin
And there we saw the men and boys
As thick as hasty puddin'

Yankee Doodle keep it up
Yankee Doodle Dandy
Mind the music and the step
And with the girls be handy

DIARY PROMPT

Have students write in their diaries about how they feel about witnessing the surrender of the British army to the Patriots. Ask the Patriots to write about how they think their lives will change as a result of winning the Revolutionary War, and have the Loyalists write about how they think their lives will change as a result of losing the war.

Wrapping Up

The day after the class has completed the simulation, engage students in a discussion, asking them to share what they've learned from their experience. After the discussion, have students write one last entry in their diaries, summarizing the entire simulation and the key events they have witnessed and been part of over the past eight years.

Use students' diary entries to assess how much students have learned about what it was like to live in the colonies and be part of the War for Independence.

Resources

BOOKS

Dorling Kindersley Eyewitness Books: American Revolution
(DK Publishing, 2002)

Liberty's Children: Stories of Eleven Revolutionary War Children
by Scotti Cohn (Globe Pequot, 2004)

My Brother Sam Is Dead
by James Lincoln Collier and Christopher Collier (Scholastic, 1974)

Johnny Tremain
by Esther Forbes (Houghton Mifflin, 1943)

The American Revolution for Kids: A History with 21 Activities
by Janis Herbert (Chicago Review Press, 2002)

Revolutionary War Days: Discover the Past With Exciting Projects, Games, Activities, and Recipes
(American Kids in History series) by David C. King (Jossey-Bass, 2001)

American Revolution: 1700–1800 (Chronicle of America)
by Joy Masoff (Scholastic, 2000)

If You Lived at the Time of the American Revolution
by Kay Moore (Scholastic, 1998)

A Young Patriot: The American Revolution as Experience by One Boy
by Jim Murphy (Clarion Books, 1996)

American Revolution: Battles and Leaders
edited by Aaron R. Murray (DK Publishing, 2004)

Time Enough for Drums
by Ann Rinaldi (Random House, 1986)

Images of the American Revolution

http://www.archives.gov/education/lessons/revolution-images/index.html

Primary Documents

Declaration of Independence

http://www.ushistory.org/declaration/document/index.htm

http://www.archives.gov/national-archives-experience/charters/declaration_transcript.html

http://www.archives.gov/historical-docs/document.html?doc=1&title.raw=Declaration%20of%20Independence

The Virginia Declaration of Rights

http://www.archives.gov/national-archives-experience/charters/virginia_declaration_of_rights.html

Documents from the Continental Congress and the Constitutional Convention

http://memory.loc.gov/ammem/collections/continental/

Common Sense by Thomas Paine

http://www.ushistory.org/paine/commonsense/singlehtml.htm

http://www.constitution.org/tp/comsense.htm

Letters from a Pennsylvania Farmer

http://www.earlyamerica.com/earlyamerica/bookmarks/farmer/farmtext.html

http://teachingamericanhistory.org/library/index.asp?subcategory=17

http://odur.let.rug.nl/~usa/D/1751-1775/townshend/dickII.htm

From Revolution to Reconstruction: Documents: Waldo's Diary, 1777

http://odur.let.rug.nl/~usa/D/1776-1800/war/waldo.htm

From Revolution to Reconstruction: Documents: Denny's Diary, 1781

http://odur.let.rug.nl/~usa/D/1776-1800/war/denny.htm

Barker, John. The British on Boston. Cambridge, MA: Harvard University Press, 1924.

http://pds.lib.harvard.edu/pds/view/2581128

About the Loyalists

American Loyalists

http://www.redcoat.me.uk/index.htm

Loyalist Institute Home Page

http://www.royalprovincial.com/

Loyalists During the American Revolution

http://www.let.rug.nl/usa/H/1994/ch3_p14.htm

American Revolution Uniforms

Continental Infantry – Patriots

http://www.srcalifornia.com/uniforms/r4.htm

2nd Massachusetts Infantry – Patriots

http://www.srcalifornia.com/uniforms/p12.htm

British 10th Regiment of Foot – Loyalists

http://www.srcalifornia.com/uniforms/p31.htm

Field Yager Corps, Hessian Mercenaries – Loyalists

http://www.srcalifornia.com/uniforms/p47.htm

American Revolution Flags

Flags of the American Revolution

http://www.foundingfathers.info/American-flag/Revolution.html

Historical Flags of the Revolutionary War

http://www.americanrevwar.homestead.com/files/FLAGS.HTM

Flags of the American Revolution

http://members.tripod.com/~txscv/revolt.htm